A l
Shefi
p

One Day When We Were Young

by Nick Payne

The first performance of
One Day When We Were Young
took place on 5 October 2011
at the Crucible Studio Theatre, Sheffield.

One Day When We Were Young

by Nick Payne

Cast

VIOLET	**Maia Alexander**
LEONARD	**Andrew Sheridan**

Creative Team

Direction	**Clare Lizzimore**
Design	**Lucy Osborne**
Lighting	**Emma Chapman**
Sound	**Adrienne Quartly**
Assistant Direction	**Titas Halder**
Make-up Artist	**Sylvia Polka**
Costume Supervisor	**Debbie Gamble**
Dialect and Voice Coach	**Michaela Kennan**
Production Manager	**Bernd Fauler**
Stage Manager	**Sarah Caselton-Smith**
Deputy Stage Manager	**Mary Hely**
Assistant Stage Manager	**Louise Martin**
Set Builder	**Factory Settings**

Sets and costumes by Sheffield Theatres
workshop and wardrobe departments

Company

Maia Alexander | Violet

Maia trained at RADA.

Productions whilst at RADA include; *All About My Mother, The Crucible, The Young Idea, The Workroom.*

Andrew Sheridan | Leonard

Andrew trained at Rose Bruford College

Theatre credits include: *A Thousand Stars Explode in the Sky* by David Eldridge (Lyric Hammersmith); *Antigone, Jonah and Otto* by Robert Holman, *The Rise and Fall of Little Voice, Across Oka, The Ribcage, Port* by Simon Stephens (Manchester Royal Exchange); *Holes in the Skin* by Robert Holman (Chichester Minerva); *Skinned* (Nuffield Southampton).

Film and Television credits include: *Control* (Momentum Pictures), *Heartbeat, Kingdom, Cold Blood, Coronation St, New Street Law, Shameless, Buried, Night Flight, Urban Gothic, Clocking Off.*

Andrew's first play *Winterlong* won the 2008 Bruntwood Playwriting Competition and premiered at the Manchester Royal Exchange in 2011 before transferring to The Soho Theatre London.

Nick Payne | Writer

Plays for the theatre include: *Sophocles' Electra* (Gate Theatre); *Wanderlust* (Royal Court Theatre); *If There Is I Haven't Found It Yet* (Bush Theatre). Forthcoming: *Lay Down Your Cross* (Hampstead Theatre). Radio credits include: *The Day We Caught The Train* (BBC Radio 4).

Winner of the 2009 George Devine Award for Most Promising Playwright. Currently under commission to the Manhattan Theatre Club/Alfred P Sloan Foundation to write a new play about maths, science or technology. www.curtisbrown.co.uk/nick-payne

Clare Lizzimore | Direction

Clare is an award-winning theatre director. Her credits include *Pieces of Vincent* by David Watson (Arcola Theatre), *Faces in the Crowd* by Leo Butler (Royal Court Theatre), *War and Peace, Fear and Misery* by Mark Ravenhill (Royal Court Theatre and Latitude Festival), *On the Rocks* by Amy Rosenthal (Hampstead Theatre), *Jonah and Otto* by Robert Holman (Royal Exchange Theatre, Manchester), *Tom Fool* (Glasgow Citizens Theatre and Bush Theatre), *The Most Humane Way to Kill A Lobster* by Duncan Macmillan (Theatre 503) and, as Co-Director with Max Stafford Clark, *The Mother* (Royal Court Theatre). Lizzimore has also directed new plays from Russia, Nigeria, Portugal and Romania, and travelled extensively for the Royal Court Theatre's International Programme, developing new plays with artists in Africa and The Middle East. Her awards include the Channel 4 Theatre Directors Award 2005/06 and the Arts Foundation Theatre Directing Fellowship 2009 for innovation. She is Co-Artistic director of Pieces Productions with David Watson (Paines Plough Associate Company) and Associate Director at Hampstead Theatre where she will be directing Nick Payne's next play *Lay Down Your Cross*.

Lucy Osborne | Design

Recent theatre credits include: *Love, Love, Love* by Mike Bartlett (Paines Plough); *The Taming of the Shrew* and *Twelfth Night* (for which she won Chicago 'Jeff Award' for Scenic Design) for the Chicago Shakespeare Theatre; *Plenty, The Long and the Short and The Tall* (Sheffield Theatres); *Precious Little Talent* by Ella Hickson (Trafalgar Studios); *Playhouse Live: Here* by Eve Ensler (Sky Arts); *Anderson's English* by Sebastian Barry, *Dreams of Violence* by Stella Feehily (Out of Joint); *Shades* by Alia Bano for the Royal Court's Young Writers Festival; *Macbeth* (Edinburgh Lyceum/Nottingham Playhouse); *Timing* (Kings Head) and *When Romeo Met Juliet* (BBC). Forthcoming productions include *Huis Clos* for the Donmar Warehouse season at Trafalgar Studios.

Lucy is an Associate Artist at the Bush Theatre and her designs there include *Where's My Seat?*, *The Aliens* by Annie Barker, *Like a Fishbone and 2,000 Feet Away* by Anthony Weigh , *The Whisky Taster* by James Graham, *If There Is I Haven't Found It Yet* by Nick Payne, *Wrecks* by Neil LaBute, *Broken Space Festival*, *Sea Wall* by Simon Stephens, *Tinderbox* by Lucy Kirkwood and *tHe dYsFUnCKshOnalZ!* by Mike Packer.

She designed *Artefacts* by Mike Bartlett (nabokov / Bush) and *Some Kind of Bliss* by Samuel Adamson (Trafalgar Studios), both of which transferred to the 2008 'Brits off Broadway Festival' in New York and other theatre credits include *Be My Baby* by Amanda Whittington (New Vic Theatre); *Rope* (Watermill Theatre); *Closer* (Theatre Royal Northampton); *The Prayer Room* by Shan Khan (Birmingham Rep/Edinburgh Festival); *Ship of Fools* by Andrew Bovell (set, Theatre 503); *The Unthinkable* by Steve Waters (Sheffield Crucible Studio); and *Season of Migration to the North* (RSC New Writing Season).

Lucy graduated from Motley Theatre Design School in 2003, having also gained a BA in Fine Art from the University of Newcastle.

Emma Chapman | Lighting

Emma trained at Bristol Old Vic Theatre School.

Theatre credits in 2011 include: *Rose* by Hywel John (Edinburgh Festival), *Cosi Fan Tutte* (Royal College of Music), *All About My Mother* (RADA), *Dangerous Corner* (Bury St Edmunds), *The Machine Gunners* (Polka Theatre), *Bus Stop* (Stoke and Scarborough) and *The Painter* by Rebecca Lenkiewicz opening the new Arcola Theatres;

Theatre credits in 2010 include: *Carmen* (Royal Northern College), *Blowing* (Cambridge and tour), *The Maddening Rain* by Nicholas Pierpan (Old Red Lion), Frantic Assembly at the artsdepot; The Young Vic Schools' *Theatre Festival*.

Previous productions include several plays at Trafalgar Studios amongst them the multiple award winning *The Mountaintop* by Katori Hall.

She has worked in many regional British theatres, colleges and other venues and in many of London's foremost fringe theatres lighting a wide variety of repertoire including several Shakespeare plays, opera, musicals, revue and new writing.

Work in progress: *Coasting* by Natalie McGrath (Bristol Old Vic), *Dick Whittington* (Bury St Edmunds) and *Dublin Carol* (Donmar at the Trafalgar season).

www.emmachapman.co.uk

Adrienne Quartly | Sound

Theatre credits include: *The Importance of Being Earnest/Farewell to the Theatre* by Richard Nelson (The Rose, Kingston) *And the Horse you rode in on* (Told by an Idiot, Barbican); *Chekov in Hell* by Dan Rebellato (Soho/Drum Plymouth); *Fräuline Julie* (Katie Mitchell at the Schaübuhne and at the Auvergne Festival 2011); *Stockholm* by Bryony Lavery (Frantic Assembly/Sydney Theatre Co.); *Thomas Hobbes* by Adriano Shaplin and *Mary Spindler* by Phil Porter (Royal Shakespeare Company); *The Container* by Clare Bayley (Young Vic); *365* by David Harrower (National Theatre of Scotland); *Woyzeck* (St. Anns Warehouse, New York);*The Painter* by Rebecca Lenkiewicz (New Arcola); *Reykjavik* (Shaw Theatre, Roundhouse), *My Zinc Bed, Private Fears* by Alan Ayckbourn; *Just between Ourselves* (Royal and Derngate, Northampton); *93.2FM* by Levi David Addai (Royal Court Theatre); *Fastest Clock in the Universe* (Hampstead); *Grand Guignol* by Carl Grose, *Nostalgia* by Lucinda Coxon (Drum Plymouth); *Dream Story, Tejas Verdes* (Gate); *Mrs Reynolds and the Ruffian* by Gary Owen (Watford Palace); *Hysteria* (Inspector Sands).

Composing credits include: *Thomas Hobbes* (RSC); *Duchess of Malfi/Faustus/Volpone/School for Scandal* (Stage on Screen); *The Painter, Enemy of the People* (Arcola). Coming up: *You can't take it with you* (Told by an idiot, Royal Exchange).

Titas Halder | Assistant Direction

Titas Halder is a director and playwright. He was Resident Assistant Director at the Donmar Warehouse (2010-2011), Creative Associate at the Bush Theatre, and Literary Associate at the Finborough Theatre. He trained with the Royal Court Theatre Young Writers' Programme. Directing includes: *Write to Rock* (Clwyd Theatr Cymru), *Painting a Wall* by David Lan (Finborough Theatre).

Paines Plough

'A major force for new writing'
The Guardian

Paines Plough is an award-winning, nationally and internationally renowned touring theatre company, specialising exclusively in commissioning and producing new plays and helping playwrights develop their craft.

'If new writing in this country is going to have any far-reaching significance, then it needs the touring company Paines Plough'
The Independent

As the UK's national theatre of new plays with the playwright always at the heart of everything we do, Paines Plough widely tours world premiere productions and offers bespoke development support to playwrights.

Paines Plough was founded in 1974. It was named after the beer its founders were drinking (Paines bitter) and the pub in which they were drinking it (The Plough) at the moment the company was conceived.

Over the past 37 years, Paines Plough has established itself as a leading new writing company producing work by a wide range of playwrights across the UK and abroad. We've produced more than 100 new productions by world renowned playwrights like Stephen Jeffreys, Abi Morgan, Sarah Kane, Mark Ravenhill, Dennis Kelly and Mike Bartlett.

The current Artistic Directors James Grieve and George Perrin took up post in 2010 with a mission to produce more plays, in more places, then ever before. Whether you're in Liverpool or Luton or Lincoln; Nottingham, Newcastle or Newbury; Bristol, Brighton or Belfast, a Paines Plough show will be in a theatre near you soon.

Paines Plough were the winners of The Stage Award for Outstanding Achievement in Regional Theatre at the TMA Awards 2010.

'Paines Plough has hit new heights since Grieve and Perrin took over as artistic directors.
The company's output has been astonishing – the pair's inaugural season saw them tour 9 new plays to 33 towns and cities across the UK.'
The Stage

At Paines Plough

Artistic Directors **James Grieve**
George Perrin
Producer **Tara Wilkinson**
General Manager **Claire Simpson**
Administrator **Hanna Streeter**
Production Manager **Bernd Fauler**
Trainee Producer (Step Change) **Rachel Quinney**
Admin Intern **Amy Michaels**

Board of Directors

Ola Animashawun, Christopher Bath, Tamara Cizeika, Chris Elwell, Marilyn Imrie, Nia Janis, Zarine Kharas, Caro Newling (Chair), Clare O'Brien

Contact Hanna Streeter, Paines Plough
4th Floor, 43 Aldwych, London, WC2B 4DN
T +44 (0) 20 7240 4533 | fax +44 (0) 20 7240 4534
office@painesplough.com | www.painesplough.com

Follow @PainesPlough on Twitter
Add Paines Plough on Facebook
Sign up to our newsletter at **www.painesplough.com**

Paines Plough and Sheffield Theatres would like to thank
the following for their support on the production:

Zippo UK
Manchester Royal Exchange
Hull Truck Theatre
Julian Middleton of RHWL Architects
vegancakedirect.co.uk
Specsavers Hearing Centre
Crystal Peaks Shopping Centre Sheffield
Seven Oaks Sound and Vision Sheffield
Paul Radford of NHS Sheffield Teaching Hospitals
Supplies & Commercial Services

The Roundabout Season

The Auditorium

For the first time in Paines Plough's 37 year history, we're building our own theatre. In partnership with Sheffield Theatres, we're creating the UK's first small-scale in-the-round touring amphitheatre. We're calling it The Roundabout Auditorium.

We think theatre-in-the-round is one of the most exhilarating ways to watch theatre – the original and best 3D experience. As leading British playwright Simon Stephens says:

What I cherish about theatre is that it gives us an insight in to what it is to be a human being – there's no theatrical architecture that challenges or interrogates what it is to be a human being more than theatre-in-the-round.

With only five in-the-round theatres in the UK, most people have never had the chance to see work in this most exciting and intimate of environments.

As a new writing touring company our aim is to make the best contemporary plays available to everyone, irrespective of geography, in high quality productions and exciting performance contexts. This is why we came up with the idea of creating The Roundabout Auditorium, and why its ease of portability is key to its success as a revolutionary concept in touring theatre.

It will flat pack into a lorry and pop-up anywhere from the stages of main house theatres, to arts centres and studio theatres, eventually touring to village halls, schools, warehouses and parks in every corner of the UK. From Liverpool to Lyme Regis, Taunton to Trowbridge, Harrogate to Harlow – The Roundabout Auditorium will turn up on the doorsteps of audiences everywhere and ensures everyone has the same extraordinary experience.

We hope its legacy will be years of world-beating plays, performed in a unique and electric setting, in top quality Paines Plough productions by a raft of the most exciting UK playwrights.

The auditorium is designed by **Lucy Osborne**, with lighting by **Emma Chapman**.

The Season

To launch the concept Paines Plough and Sheffield Theatres have programmed this inaugural **Roundabout Season,** which sees three world premières of new plays by **Nick Payne**, **Duncan Macmillan** and **Penelope Skinner**. The last play in the season, by Penelope Skinner, has been specifically commissioned for the acting ensemble.

The Roundabout Season opened at the Crucible Studio, Sheffield – as part of the company's 40th anniversary season – on 5 October 2011.

We believe The Roundabout Auditorium will fundamentally transform the new writing touring landscape in the UK. But we need the help of people who share our passion for new plays, touring and groundbreaking new ideas.

You can support us through: justgiving.com/painesplough

Sheffield Theatres

Sheffield Theatres is the largest producing theatre complex outside London. With three theatres: the Lyceum, the Crucible and the Studio, Sheffield presents a diverse programme of work including drama, dance, comedy, musicals, opera, ballet and children's shows.

In February 2010 the Crucible reopened following a £15.3 million redevelopment programme. Under the Artistic Directorship of Daniel Evans, the Theatres have since presented three seasons of critically acclaimed, in-house produced work in both the Crucible and the Studio, including **An Enemy of the People** with Sir Antony Sher, Polly Stenham's **That Face** with a cast including Frances Barber, **Hamlet** with John Simm, the musical **Me and My Girl** and a season of work celebrating playwright David Hare.

The Roundabout Season is the first time that Sheffield Theatres and Paines Plough have collaborated.

In November 2011, the Crucible will turn 40 and is embarking on a year-long celebration of its birthday, launching a host of initiatives to help to raise funds for its future. Over the next twelve months the theatre will stage a host of productions and events inspired by its reputation for staging great classic plays and dazzling musicals; its commitment to developing artistic talent and offering a place for local artists to explore the arts and its ambition to remain at the heart of the country's cultural life.

The Crucible began its 40th birthday season with **One Monkey Don't Stop No Show**, a co-production with Eclipse Theatre in the Studio, and its first ever production of Shakespeare's **Othello** on the Crucible stage, with Dominic West and Clarke Peters. The birthday season will continue with a host of events in November 2011 to mark the Crucible's birthday, including **Fanfared** a special interactive tour of the building inspired by the first production on stage in 1971, and the first play from the newly formed Sheffield People's Theatre, **Lives in Art**. **Stephen Sondheim**'s **Company** will end the first part of the 40th celebrations in December.

sheffieldtheatres.co.uk

Chief Executive **Dan Bates**
Artistic Director **Daniel Evans**
Business Resources Director **Bookey Oshin**
Commercial Director **Roxy Daniells**
Sales and Communications Director **Claire Murray**

Supported by
ARTS COUNCIL ENGLAND

Relive 40 dramatic years with our new book

1971 - 2011

CRUCIBLE 40

To celebrate our 40th birthday, we've compiled a chronicle of the Crucible's history. This fascinating and colourful volume includes photographs, programme covers, posters and many memories from four remarkable decades of theatre.

Since its opening in 1971, the Crucible has attracted regional, national and international attention. From the controversy which surrounded the original design of its thrust stage to the pioneering work of its theatre-in-education department, Vangard; from its world premières to its lavish musicals; from its community ensembles to its internationally renowned casts, the Crucible Theatre has played an essential role in Sheffield's life for over 40 years.

Crucible 40 tells this iconic theatre's story so far.

Crucible 40 is now available to purchase from Sheffield Theatres, priced at £25.00

Box Office 0114 249 6000
sheffieldtheatres.co.uk

Factory Settings

Factory Settings are very pleased to be working again with Paines Plough and Sheffield Theatres.

From simple beginnings six years ago operating from the Pleasance London workshop, Will Jackson and Lucien Mansell have steadily grown Factory Settings to become an ISO:9001 registered company serving the theatre and exhibitions industries, with clients ranging from small fringe companies right through to the Royal Opera House, National Theatre, and Victoria and Albert Museum.

Our capabilities have recently increased further with the acquisition of more suitable premises just a mile down the road from our previous accommodation in Leyton, East London.

The company's ongoing steady growth has always been tempered by our love of theatre and design, and a desire to keep enjoying the people, the product, and the cooperative creative process of realising theatre works.

We are always happy to talk about projects and ideas, no matter what stage they are at, so feel free to get in touch.

T:0208 988 1418
info@factorysettings.co.uk
www.factorysettings.co.uk

Nick Payne
One Day
When We Were Young

faber and faber

First published in 2011
by Faber and Faber Ltd
74–77 Great Russell Street
London WC1B 3DA

Typeset by Country Setting, Kingsdown, Kent CT14 8ES
Printed in England by CPI Group (UK) Ltd, Croydon CR0 4YY

A CIP record for this book
is available from the British Library

978–0–571–28395–8

2 4 6 8 10 9 7 5 3 1

For my Grandparents

Acknowledgements

Clare Lizzimore.

James Grieve, George Perrin, Tara Wilkinson and all of the staff at Paines Plough. Ruth Carney, Daniel Evans and all of the staff at Sheffield Theatres.

Maia Alexander, Siân Brooke, Dominique Bull, Samuel Collings, Cliff Densley, John Evans, Jane Fallowfield, Lou Finn, Elizabeth Freestone, Nicholas Gleaves, Titas Halder, Victor Lawrence, Duncan Macmillan, Anna Madeley, Morgan Lloyd Malcolm, Andrew Muir, Andrew Scott, Andrew Sheridan, Clare Slater, Al Smith, Frank Sumison, Nina Steiger, Rachael Stevens, Rachel Wagstaff and Jenny Worton.

Ben Hall and Lily Williams at Curtis Brown.

Lastly, I would like to acknowledge the following books and their authors: *Europe at War* by Norman Davies, *Bath at War* by Jonathan Falconer and David Falconer, *Among the Dead Cities* by A. C. Grayling, *Twenty-One* by James Holland, *The Railway Man* by Eric Lomax, *A History of Modern Britain* by Andrew Marr, *Never Had it So Good* by Dominic Sandbrook, *Memoirs of an Infantry Officer* by Siegfried Sassoon, *Wartime Women* edited by Dorothy Sheridan, *Three Star Blitz* by Charles Whiting and *Soldiers* by Philip Ziegler.

Characters

Leonard
born in London, 1924

Violet
born in Bath, 1925

ONE DAY WHEN WE WERE YOUNG

'History without compassion is a very empty vessel'
Norman Davies, *Europe at War*

*An ellipsis (. . .) following a character's name
indicates a desire to speak but an inability
to know quite what to say.*

*An ellipsis (. . .) on its own indicates a pause,
a beat, a silence.*

One

Bath, 25 April 1942.
   A room in the Hotel Regina, around 10.30 p.m.
   Leonard and Violet asleep in their respective single beds. Their clothes folded neatly on the floor beside their beds.
   The room is extremely dark, only natural light.
   Leonard wakes suddenly.
   Leonard gets out of bed, moves to his clothes and takes from them a packet of cigarettes and a box of matches.
   Leonard lights a cigarette.
   Leonard moves to the window.
   Violet wakes slowly.
   Violet spots Leonard at the window.

Violet What are you looking at?

Leonard You're awake.

Violet I am.

Leonard I'm sorry.

Violet Don't be.

Leonard Mean I'm sorry if I woke you.

Violet Were you looking at the moon?

Leonard No.

Violet Is there something the matter?

Leonard No.
   I'm sorry.

Violet (*shakes her head a little*) Would you like to come back to bed?

Leonard In a moment maybe.

Violet Why don't I turn the light on?

Leonard No, don't.

Violet gets out of bed.

Violet Is it the bed, do you think?

Leonard The bed?

Violet That's keeping you awake.

Leonard I don't think it's the bed, no.

Violet Maybe we should swap beds.

Leonard Violet, I –

Violet Honestly.
This is the bed for you, I think.

Leonard . . .

*Violet moves to Leonard, gently takes his hand and
walks him back towards her bed.*
Violet pulls back the sheets.
Leonard gets into (Violet's) bed.
Violet gets into (Leonard's) bed.

Violet How's that?

Leonard Hard to say.

Violet Does it feel any better?

Leonard Not particularly, no.

Violet Maybe it's the room. Why don't I go and see –

Leonard It's not the –

Violet No, why don't I go and see if they have another –

Leonard It's not the room.
  It's a lovely room.
  It's a lovely room.

Violet Would you like to play a game of whist?

Leonard No.

Violet Have you tried counting sheep?

Leonard Perhaps if neither of us says anything for a moment.

. . .

Violet I do love this ceiling.

Leonard gets out of bed, moves.

I'm sorry.
  What would you like me to do?

Leonard Nothing.
  Honestly.

Violet Your feet; it's bound to be your feet.

Leonard My feet?

Violet Those shoes you have are so old –

Leonard My shoes?

Violet Not fit for walking, let alone dancing.
  Let me rub them.

Leonard What?

Violet Your feet.

Leonard I might just go for a walk.

Violet A walk?

Leonard Just briefly.

Violet It's late.

Leonard I know.

Violet You'll only be told to come back in.

Leonard I won't be long.

Leonard moves to his clothes and begins getting dressed.

Violet Leonard, please don't go for a walk. Please.

Leonard stops getting dressed.

Tell me what it is. That's the matter.

Leonard . . .
I was having a dream. And it woke me up.

Violet What was it about?

Leonard Why don't you come with me?

Violet What was the dream about, Leonard?

Leonard . . .
Father Christmas.

Violet Father Christmas?

Leonard Father Christmas.

Violet Just the two of you?

Leonard ?

Violet In the dream.

Leonard Right.

Violet It was just the two of you, was it?

Leonard Yes.

Violet What was he doing?
Father Christmas, what was he –?

Leonard I was trapped.

Violet Trapped?

Leonard Yes, trapped. In the ground. Mud.
Sinking.
I was in it up to my knees and there didn't seem to be anybody else around.
And then, in the distance, I noticed.

Violet Father Christmas.

Leonard I noticed Father Christmas.
I started shouting. For help.
He didn't seem to hear me so I, I cupped my hands around my mouth and I shouted a bit louder.
He comes towards me, comes right to me and he offers me his hand.
I, I grab his hand and he pulls me out.

Violet Saved.

Leonard I wipe the mud from my trousers and, when I look up again, to say thank you, I realise it's not actually.

Violet Father Christmas.

Leonard I realise it's not actually Father Christmas at all.

Violet Who is it?

Leonard He's Japanese.

Violet Father Christmas is Japanese?

Leonard No, it's not him.

Violet It's not –

Leonard Not any more, no. Not once I'm out of the mud.

Violet Oh.
What happens once you realise it's not really –?

Leonard I wake up.

Violet . . .

Leonard It's all right.
I'm all right.

Violet moves, reaches under (her) bed and pulls out a cake tin.

Violet This was supposed to be a surprise for the morning.

Violet holds out the cake tin for Leonard.

Open it.

Leonard What is it?

Leonard takes the cake tin from Violet and removes the lid.

Violet I made it, but it's not just from me. It's also from Mother and Father and Louise.
We didn't have any cream – no one had any cream.
All I mean is, I know it might look like cream and hopefully it might taste like cream, but it's actually water and margarine mixed with a little powdered milk and a touch of vanilla essence.
It's from everyone. The whole street.
Everyone's really proud of you, Leonard.

Leonard Thank you.

Violet Wouldn't you like to try some?

Leonard I thought you said it was for the morning?
Don't mind waiting.

Violet Oh.

Leonard Mean I'm happy to wait. If that's what you want.
Mean if that's what you had in mind, I'm happy to –

Leonard breaks off a piece of cake with his hand and eats.

   Violet watches Leonard.

(*Mouth full of food.*) It's lovely.

   Violet is smiling; Leonard has some cream on his nose.

What?

Violet You've got . . . cream on your nose.

   *Violet wipes the cream from Leonard's nose.
   Leonard replaces the lid on the cake tin.*

Leonard Thank you.

Violet Glad you like it.

Leonard I do.
   Thank you.

Violet What for?

Leonard Tonight.
   Taking me out.

Violet What did you tell your mother?
   About not coming home.

Leonard I told her that I was going dancing and that I was going to stay at Patrick's house.
   You?

Violet I left a note.

Leonard You're joking?

   Violet shakes her head.

What did it say?

Violet That we were going to the Hotel Regina to spend our last night together.

And that it was extremely likely that I wouldn't be home again until the morning.

But they mustn't worry because –

Leonard kisses Violet.
  They separate.

Are you –?

Leonard kisses Violet.
  They separate.

Leonard This isn't actually going to be our last night together. Is it?

Violet Of course not, I didn't mean –

Leonard The way you said it then, though, you made it sound as if –

Violet I meant for the time being.

Leonard Coming back, though.

Violet I know.

Leonard As soon as it's all over –

Violet I know.
  (*Soft.*) I know.

Leonard I mean it.

Violet As do I.

Leonard Good. Good.

Because if there's one thing I don't want tonight to be it's a night of.

And don't take this the wrong way because I've had a lovely evening. I really have.

But, if I'm honest, I think the reason I'm having trouble sleeping is because.

It's not the dancing, not my shoes, my feet.

This whole evening, everything we've done, the, the, the, picnic, the dance, the walk, this room –

Violet Leonard –

Leonard I am actually incredibly scared.
And not how you might think.
I am scared, that once this war is over, and I am sent home, that you won't be here.
That you might be gone.

Violet Leonard –

Leonard Because who knows how long I might be –

Violet I don't care.

Leonard But –

Violet I really don't.

Leonard How long, though?

Violet What?

Leonard To wait. How long would you be willing to wait?

Violet As long as it takes.

Leonard Ten years?

Violet I –

Leonard Eleven? Twelve?

Violet It's not going to be –

Leonard We could be old.
I could be an old man.

Violet I like old men.

Leonard That's what I'm worried about.

Violet That was a joke.

Leonard There's a woman, Mrs Evans, I deliver to her every Saturday. Always has the same thing.

Bones. All she ever has.

Makes stocks, she says. Soups.

Last weekend I knock on her door as normal, but there's no answer.

I knock again but still no answer.

I'm about to leave when I hear her voice from inside call out my name.

Leonard, she says, is that you? It's me I say, it's me.

I've cut my hand she says. Would I mind coming inside and helping her, she says.

I go in and she has a blood-soaked tea towel wrapped around her thumb.

The point being is that while I'm sitting with her waiting for the bleeding to stop I end up telling her that I've been called up and that I'm due to leave within the week.

She tells me that her husband used to be a soldier.

Oh really, I say?

Conscript, she says, yes, same as me.

I'd love to meet him, I say.

He's dead, she says, but if you're interested I could certainly show you some of his belongings, she says.

He, he kept a diary.

Leonard moves to his pile of clothes on the floor beside the bed and removes from them a small pocket diary.

When I arrived back at the shop, I asked Neil if he'd ever known Mrs Evans's husband.

Yes, he says, very well in fact. Both before and after the war.

After the war? But I thought he died during?

No, he says. All happened after.

Leonard opens the diary, flicks to a particular page and reads:

'I can't help feeling more and more that this war has become mechanical and inhuman. We have gone from drafts of volunteers to droves of victims in the space of a year.'

He flicks to a different page, reads:

'. . . The face was grey and waxen, with a stiff little moustache; he looked like a doll, grotesque and undignified. Beside him was a scorched and mutilated figure whose contorted attitude revealed his bristly cheeks, grinning blood-smeared mouth and clenched teeth. These dead were unlike our own.'

He jumped from his own roof.

Mr Evans.

Violet Why would you want to read that to me?

Leonard I cannot stop thinking about it.

Violet Would you mind if I went to the toilet?

Leonard Course not.

Violet Thank you.

Exit Violet.
Leonard moves to the cake tin, lifts the lid and breaks off another piece of cake.
Enter Violet.

On Monday when I arrived at the shop, there was the most enormous queue of people.

Dad had managed to lay his hands on a number of chocolate bars and word had got round.

We tried to see to everyone as quickly as we could, but the queue just seemed to be getting longer and longer.

All of sudden there seemed to be a particularly pungent odour making its way about the shop.

Everyone's noses started twitching.

All weekend I had been thinking about you. And about what I might say when it comes to saying goodbye.

I am so anxious about seeing you off that I have been breaking wind almost non-stop since Monday.

Leonard Violet –

Violet I am just as nervous and I am just as scared as you are.
  But I do not think that it is fair of you to question how long I may or may not be willing to wait.
  Nor do I think that it is very graceful of you to have taken that poor man's diary.

Leonard Violet, come away with me.

Violet What?

Leonard Come away with me.

Violet I don't understand?

Leonard Let's leave.
  Together.

Violet Leave?

Leonard Yes.

Violet You mean leave Bath?

Leonard I mean leave Bath.

Violet You mean now?

Leonard Yes.

Violet Tonight?

Leonard I mean now, tonight.

Violet Leonard, please, be serious –

Leonard I am.

Violet What would your mother say?

Leonard We could find somewhere by the sea.

Violet The sea?

Leonard A house. The two of us.

Violet I think perhaps you should stop talking.

Leonard Why?
Why?
Given half a chance, tell me you wouldn't want to.
Somewhere new.
Remote.
Untouched by war.

Violet Leonard, I really think we should –

Leonard Hypothetically. Given the chance –

Violet I think you should give me that diary.

Leonard Violet –

Violet No. I am sorry.
But.
This is my home.
This is my home.

Leonard Marry me then.

Violet . . .
What?

Leonard . . .

Violet takes the diary from Leonard, replaces the lid on the cake tin and moves.
She places the cake tin underneath (her) bed and puts the diary into a drawer on the bedside table.
Violet begins refolding Leonard's clothes on the floor.

Violet I think you're being incredibly selfish.
Actually.
Thoughtless.

And I don't like it.
I'm worried as well, you know.
Of course I don't *want* you to go.
And of course I've thought about.
Leaving. But.
No. Leonard. No.

Violet watches Leonard.
She grows upset.

I hope to be able to spend the rest of my life with you.
Do you understand?

Leonard moves to the bedside table and switches on
the bedside lamp.
Leonard moves to Violet, close.

Leonard When I get back, I am going to buy us a house.

Violet You don't have to buy –

Leonard And I am going to open my own butcher's shop.
And once rationing is over, we'll sell only the prime cuts.
   And once we have a house, and if we have enough
money, I think we should buy a grand piano.
   And once we have a grand piano I think you should
teach me how to play it.
   What do you think?

Violet Why don't we get back into bed?

Violet moves as if for the bed but Leonard gently stops
her.

Something the matter?

Leonard moves to Violet, close.
He kisses Violet.
He suddenly picks Violet up from around her waist
and carries her, at pace, to the bed.
Violet now stands on the bed, Leonard on the floor,
looking up.

Leonard I meant what I said.
About.
I really would.

Violet I don't understand?

Leonard Marry you.
I don't know a single person a bit like you, Violet.

Violet begins jumping on the bed.

What are you doing?

Violet I don't know.

Leonard climbs up on to the bed.
   He begins jumping on the bed also.
   Leonard and Violet now both jump up and down on the bed, getting progressively higher and higher each time – perhaps nearly reaching the ceiling even.
   Leonard and Violet stop jumping, and Violet, sternly yet playfully, places Leonard's arms around her, as if readying the two of them for a waltz.
   Leonard perhaps laughs a little and attempts to break the position.
   Violet persists.
   She begins to hum the opening bars of 'One Day When We Were Young'.
   Violet and Leonard attempt to waltz on the bed.
   Violet begins to sing 'One Day When We Were Young'.
   Violet gestures for Leonard to join in.
   Leonard, reluctantly, begins to sing along with Violet.
   Their singing is quiet, intimate, and not at all performative.
   They stop.

I will wait for as long as you need me to.

Leonard kisses Violet.
Leonard and Violet continue to kiss, somewhat intensely.
Leonard delicately lifts Violet's slip above her head, removing it.
Violet now wears only her underwear.
Violet unfastens and removes Leonard's belt.
Leonard removes his trousers.
He now wears only his underwear.
Leonard and Violet are now horizontal on the bed.

Why don't you turn off the light?

Leonard moves to the bedside table and switches off the bedside lamp.
Leonard and Violet continue to kiss.
After a moment, the distant whistle of an incendiary bomb is heard.
Again, the distant whistle of a (different) incendiary bomb is heard, this time slightly closer.
Leonard stops kissing.

Is something the matter?

The distant sound of an incendiary hitting its target is heard.
Leonard slowly gets out of bed and begins moving towards the window.
Again, the distant sound of an incendiary hitting its target is heard.

Leonard Violet, I think something is happening.

Violet Leonard, come back to bed.

Suddenly the sound of a German aircraft is heard as it flies directly above the hotel.
Violet sits up in bed.

Leonard Get dressed.

Violet What is it, what's happening?

Leonard Will you put your clothes on, please.

*The sound of an incendiary bomb hitting its target,
now considerably closer.*
   Bath's air-raid sirens begin to ring out.

Violet, please!

*Leonard and Violet frantically begin putting their
clothes on.*
   *The sound of the German aircraft overhead and
their incendiaries, their impact, continues throughout
the remainder of the scene.*

Violet Maybe we should stay here?

Leonard What?

Violet Under the bed.

Leonard We can't.

Violet It might be safer.

Leonard The hotel must have a shelter.

Violet I don't know.

Leonard What?

Violet I don't know!

*Suddenly the window in the room is shattered, spilling
inwards, as the hotel is hit.*
   Violet screams.
   *The noise from outside, the chaos, now spills into
the room.*
   *Violet has collapsed into a ball on the floor, against
the wall.*

Leonard Violet, please, we have to go, we have to go.
   Violet, please!

Violet Perhaps we should wait and see.

Leonard What?

Violet What happens, perhaps it would be better –

Leonard Violet, please –

Violet I don't want to have to go outside.

Leonard What?

Violet I don't want to have to go outside!
    I don't want to have to –

Leonard Listen to me, listen to me –

Violet I would rather that we wait here and that we see
what happens.
    We could do that, couldn't we?
    We could wait and see.

Leonard . . .

  The noise from outside continues to flood the room.

Two

Bath, 9 February 1963.

   Royal Victoria Park, around 4 p.m.

   A large tree, stripped bare of its leaves.

   A layer of thick, white, glistening snow covers everything.

   Note: during the course of the scene, the sun should set. Also, the sound of children playing in the distance should be a constant throughout.

   Leonard sits on a bench, working on the Mirror's *daily crossword.*

   Enter Violet.

   Violet watches Leonard.

   Leonard, noticing Violet, puts his paper down on the bench and stands.

. . .

Leonard Good timing.

Violet Sorry?

Leonard Your timing. I was stuck. On two down. Driving me mad.

Violet ?

Leonard (*clarification*) Crossword. I've been stuck on the crossword.

Violet I see.

Leonard Taken me all morning.

Violet What's the clue?

Leonard . . .
  Can't believe the snow.

Violet I know.

Leonard Park looks incredible.

Violet Almost hurts your eyes if you look at it for too long.

Leonard Well they say that, don't they?

Violet Say what?

Leonard It can blind you.

Violet The snow?

Leonard Snow blindness.

. . .

I hope I didn't frighten you.
  Yesterday.

Violet Not at all, no.

Leonard You're sure?

Violet Taken aback. I was taken aback certainly. But not frightened.
  I didn't recognise you.
  I was in two minds, though, I have to confess. About coming here.

Leonard I see.

Violet I've a dinner. This evening.
  I've not long, I'm afraid.

Leonard I understand.

. . .

You were buying a washing machine?

Violet ?

Leonard Yesterday.

Violet Yes.

Leonard You were out buying a –

Violet Yes, that's right.
  We were, yes.

. . .

Leonard Any luck?

Violet Yes. Thank you.

. . .

One of our neighbours recently bought one. On credit
no less.
  I went round one afternoon. Witness its inauguration.

Leonard How was it?

Violet Sorry?

Leonard Your neighbour's washing machine. How was it?

Violet Fine. It was fine.
  Good in fact.
  We watched an entire cycle. Through the port-hole.

Leonard Right.

Violet Numb bums by the end of it.

Leonard Blimey.

Violet Anyway.

. . .

Leonard You were with your family?
  Yesterday I mean.

Violet I was, yes, that's right.
Thought for a moment you meant whilst watching the washing.

Leonard No.

Violet Suddenly thought how boring you must think we all are.

Leonard Not at all.

Violet A day out for us is an afternoon at the neighbour's watching their washing.

Leonard No, that wasn't what I meant.

Leonard and Violet smile politely at one another.

Violet Yes. You're right. I was.

Leonard Those were your children, were they?

Violet nods.

Would you mind if I ask their names?

Violet Of course I wouldn't.

. . .

Oh sorry, sorry –

Leonard No, no.

Violet I thought you meant, would you mind if I ask?
As in –

Leonard Right.

Violet As in, having asked, you were then going to –

Leonard Right, sorry, I see, no.

Violet Robert, he's sixteen. Just. Sixteen just.
And Emily, she's twelve.

Leonard Both still at school presumably?

Violet That's right.

Leonard Lovely names.

. . .

So which one did you go for?
    Washing machine. In the end.

Violet . . .

Leonard Is everything all right?

   Violet nods.

You're certain?

Violet Of course, of course.

Leonard Not too cold?

Violet No.

Leonard We could go somewhere else if you'd rather?

Violet No.

   *Violet watches Leonard, perhaps moves a little closer
   towards him.*

Are you well?

   Leonard nods.

You are?

Leonard Yes.

Violet And did you have a nice Christmas?

Leonard I did, thank you.

Violet I've seen the snow in London on the television.

Leonard Television?

Violet Sorry?

Leonard You. Television, washing machine.

Violet I see.

. . .

Leonard That was a joke. I was joking.
Don't actually live in London any more.
I have a job in Dunstable. Mum and I moved to Luton.

Violet Oh, how is your mother?

Leonard . . .

Leonard grows ever so slightly upset, but does his best to make sure it goes no further.

Cold. Making my eyes run. You don't have a tissue, do you?

Violet nods, opens her handbag and hands Leonard a handkerchief.
Leonard wipes his eyes, blows his nose.
Immediately after having blown his nose, Leonard looks at the handkerchief, wondering instantly whether he should have blown his nose into it.

God, I'm sorry.

Violet Don't be silly.

Leonard That was disgusting of me.

Violet Don't be silly.

Leonard Let me wash it for you.

Violet Leonard –

Leonard It's the least I could do.

Violet Please.

Leonard hands the snotty handkerchief back to Violet.

34

Leonard If you change your mind.

Violet puts the snotty handkerchief back into her handbag.

. . .

She passed away. Actually. Mum. Over Christmas.

Violet I am so sorry.

Leonard Thank you.

Violet Leonard, I am so sorry.

Leonard Thank you.

Violet Was there –? Had she been –?

Leonard Not sure really.
She had been sick. She had definitely been sick.

Violet How do you mean?

Leonard Blood. Coughing up blood.

Violet My goodness.

Leonard But you know what she was like – know how stubborn she could be. Refused to see anyone. 'I've got this far without their help, thank you very much,' she used to say.
Went in to wake her one morning before work. Tea in one hand, toast in the other.
Her eyes were open but she didn't seem to be looking at anything.

Violet moves to go to Leonard but stops herself before getting too close.

Violet If there is anything I can do.

She watches Leonard.

Leonard, if there is anything I can –

Leonard Thank you.

In that case, then.

The reason I wanted to come back to Bath, actually, was to.

If you were available to come to the funeral, I think it would mean a lot to her. Or would've, I suppose. It's probably 'would've', isn't it?

. . .

If you're busy –

Violet No, no.

Leonard Would of course understand, though. Is what I'm saying.

Violet Of course I'll come. Of course I will. Just trying to work everything through.

Leonard As I say, if it's –

Violet No. No. It's not.

Just a lot to take in.

Leonard Course.

. . .

Your family, they're still all –?

Violet Oh yes, yes.

Leonard Good. Good.

I saw the shop, actually.

Violet Oh really?

Leonard Did, yes.

Violet It's been difficult.

Leonard I bet.

Violet Supermarkets.

Leonard I bet, I bet.

Violet So much has changed.

Leonard The High Street looks almost entirely different.

Violet It's incredible.
It's wonderful though, don't you think?
Jack and I, we went to London. To visit some friends of ours.
They took us to some of the most extraordinary places. Cafés and bars, absolutely full to the brim.
We drank the most wonderful coffee and ate the most wonderful food.
Espresso. Have you heard of it?
Most amazing, thick, bitter coffee from Italy. And we had ravioli.
And then, then, a minute's walk or so down the road, you find yourselves eating French sausages, followed by chocolates from Switzerland.
We spent an entire day simply talking and eating and drinking. Ten years ago, that sort of thing would have been unimaginable.
And Wimpy! Oh my goodness, have you eaten at a Wimpy?

Leonard shakes his head sheepishly.

Burgers and milkshakes and. *Knickerbocker glories.*
Somebody mentioned to Jack that they thought there was one open in Bristol. Hoping to take the children along.

Leonard Burgers?

Violet The whole thing is designed to look as if it were an American diner.

Leonard Blimey.
Do they do tea?

Violet Tea?

Leonard nods.

They do everything.

> *Suddenly a football arrives between Violet and Leonard.*
> *Leonard moves to the ball, picks it up and kicks it back towards from where it came.*

. . .

I'm trying to think of a polite way to ask you whether or not you are with anyone. But I'm having trouble.

Leonard I'd say that that was reasonably polite.
My turn now to think of a polite way of saying no.
No, Violet, I am not with anyone.

Violet I'm sorry.

Leonard Why are you sorry?

Violet . . .

Leonard Hardly your fault, is it?

Violet I know it's not.

Leonard Nothing to do with you, is it?

Violet I know.

Leonard And the idea that you should feel sorry for me –

Violet I meant sorry in the sense that –

Leonard Have you considered the possibility that some people are actually quite happy as they stand?

Violet . . .

Leonard Not all of us need. Washing machines and Italian sausages and televisions to cheer us up.

Violet I know.

Leonard And if I want to eat somewhere that serves American food, then I'll go to bleedin' America.

Violet I'm sorry.

Leonard Stop saying you are sorry!

. . .

How did you and your husband meet?

Leonard watches Violet.

I shouldn't have raised my voice.
  I shouldn't.
  Violet –

Violet In the shop. We met in the shop.
  He returned home a year before the end of the war.
  He was a pilot.
  He was very badly injured and he was returned home to Bath one year before the end of the war.
  Not long after he was home, he came into the shop to collect some things for his mother and we said hello to one another.

Leonard When did you marry?

Violet I wonder if we should talk about something else?

Leonard What else is there to talk about?

Violet watches Leonard briefly.

Violet It's no good being angry with me.

Leonard Angry with you?

Violet Yes.

Leonard 'Angry with you'?

Violet Yes.

Leonard What a peculiar thing to say.

I asked how you met. And I asked when you were married. Quite how from that you managed to get to –

Violet We were married in 1946.
  It was one of the happiest days of my life.

Leonard What does he do, your husband?

Violet Leonard –

Leonard I'm interested.
  I'm interested.

Violet He's a music teacher. He teaches music.

Leonard Do you have a piano?

Violet I'm sorry?

Leonard In your home –

Violet Should I go?

Leonard What?

Violet I feel as if – (*Stops.*)

Leonard What?
  Say it.

Violet I don't want to argue.

Leonard Good for you.

Violet I don't understand?

Leonard You said you don't want to argue.

Violet That's right.

Leonard And I was saying, well, good for you.

  Violet watches Leonard.

Violet I travelled to London, you know.
  On my own. To see your mother.

Before the wedding.

I travelled to London to make absolutely doubly sure that there had not been any further news about.

You.

I travelled to London on my own to see your mother to make absolutely doubly sure that there had not been any further news and, if not, to ask her permission.

Leonard Not sure I'm following?

Violet I cried. All afternoon.

And on the way home, I cried.

I cried so hard and so constant that my chest began to ache. Everyone started asking me if I was all right.

When I finally made it back to Bath, I couldn't breathe.

Everyone was telling me I might never see you again.

Leonard How do you mean?

Violet It wasn't a straightforward decision.

Leonard Glad to hear it.

Violet I shouldn't be meeting you. I've left the children with one of the neighbours. We're supposed to be going to a friend's house this evening.

I've not told Jack.

About you. About the two of us meeting.

I wanted to see you.

I wanted to hear about how you have been getting on.

I've thought of you.

Leonard Have you?

Violet I have. Often.

Leonard Evidently not quite often enough.

Violet Are you bitter?

Leonard Bitter?

Violet Do you resent my choice?

Leonard Blimey.

Violet What would you rather I had done?

Leonard Is that a question or are you –

Violet Hope can be a terrible thing, Leonard.
If it is all that one has been left with.

Leonard I had an image of you in my mind. You'd be amazed at how clear it was. Amazed at how it kept me going.

Violet I'm sorry I'm not what you expected.

Leonard looks up at the setting sun.

Leonard It's getting dark.

Violet I wrote to you.
I wrote letters to you. After your mother received that telegram. We were told that only the next of kin was allowed to write, so we took alternate turns. We sent them to the Red Cross and we were told, assured practically, that they would somehow find their way to you.
That telegram was so cold and formal. Did your mother ever show it to you?
The language. I can still remember it now.
It said that you were 'in Japanese hands stop'.
'Letter confirming this telegram follows stop.'
And that was it.

Leonard Do you still play the piano at all?

Violet Sorry?

Leonard The piano, do you still play it at all?

Violet I do.
I teach it actually, also.

Leonard Teach?

Violet Not in a school. I'm not an actual teacher.
After school. Young children.

Leonard You have a piano in your home then, do you?

Violet We do, yes.

Leonard Is it a grand piano?

Violet It's not, no.

Leonard I miss the sound of live music. No room in the
house at the moment. Have to make do with the radio.
I am, though, absolutely addicted to *The Archers*.
Have you ever listened to it?

Violet No.

Leonard You must.
Do you smoke?

Violet Officially, no.
Jack can't stand the smell.

*Leonard hands Violet a cigarette and lights it for her.
He lights a cigarette for himself.*

Leonard What about you?

Violet ?

Leonard The smell. What do you think of it?

Violet I adore it.

. . .

When are you travelling back? To London.

Leonard Tonight.

Violet At what time?

Leonard . . .

43

Violet watches Leonard.

Violet Leonard.
I am extraordinarily happy.
Do you understand?
I have no desire to return to those last days in April.
Leonard, do you understand what it is that I am saying?

She watches Leonard.

You will let me know about your mother's service, won't you?

Leonard I will.

Violet You must.

Leonard moves to Violet.
Leonard and Violet, close.

Leonard –

Leonard It seems to have fallen very quiet.

Violet It does.

Leonard moves to kiss Violet, but Violet moves away.

I am married.

Leonard That's right.

Violet I have two children.

Leonard You do, that's right.

Violet At home.
Waiting.

Leonard You look wonderful.
Really, really wonderful.
I haven't aged half as well as you have.

Violet Don't be silly.

Leonard and Violet, close.

I really mustn't be any longer, Leonard, I'm sorry.

Violet moves to Leonard and delicately kisses him goodbye on the cheek.
Violet and Leonard remain close for a brief moment, simply looking at one another.
Violet moves to go.

Leonard I saw you coming. I saw you walking towards me.

I pretended that I hadn't. I pretended that I was struggling with the crossword.

I wasn't. It's actually a fairly simple crossword. As it happens.

Violet Goodbye, Le —

Leonard suddenly kisses Violet.
Violet attempts to draw the kiss to a close, but Leonard resists, maintaining his grip on Violet.
Violet struggles further to draw the kiss to a close. Leonard persists.
Finally, with force, Violet separates from Leonard. Slowly, it begins to snow.

Leonard I would've waited, you know.

Were it to have been the other way around.

I would have held on.

Everything's changed. That's the trouble.

You can't just pick these things up where you left off, can you?

Violet I don't know.

Three

Luton, Bedfordshire, 14 September 2002.
   The living room of Leonard's one-bedroom, semi-detached house, around 5 p.m.
   Despite the room itself being remarkably run-down, any electrical appliances visible – television, etc. – are actually quite modern-looking.
   Violet, alone in the room, has wet hair.
   Outside, the rain is hammering down, a storm.
   After a moment, enter Leonard with a towel and a box of Jaffa Cakes.
   Leonard hands the towel to Violet.

Violet Thank you.

Leonard Really is cats and dogs.

   Violet nods a little.
     She begins rubbing her hair gently. Leonard watches.

. . .

Any better?

Violet Thank you.

Leonard Hang this up in the kitchen, if you don't mind.

Violet Of course not.

Leonard Do help yourself to a Jaffa Cake.

   Exit Leonard with towel.
     Violet opens the packet of Jaffa Cakes and eats one.
     Enter Leonard.

. . .

Was everything all right with your journey?

Violet It was, yes.

Leonard What's that?

Violet (*louder*) It was fine, thank you.

Leonard Good. Good.
    Been thinking about you, coming all this way.
    There were two very serious accidents affecting trains serving this area.

Violet I saw.

Leonard Awful really.

. . .

Would you like another Jaffa Cake?

Violet Thank you.

Leonard No Value Added Tax.

Violet Sorry?

Leonard No Value Added Tax.

Violet Oh.

Leonard Biscuits and cakes. Exempt from Value Added Tax.

Violet I had no idea.

Leonard Caused a bit of a hoo-ha actually.

Violet Really?

Leonard 1991. Her Majesty's Customs and Excise tried to reclassify the Jaffa Cake as a chocolate-covered biscuit.
    And if you're a chocolate-covered biscuit, you have to pay your Value Added Tax.

Violet Well.

Leonard Took the Jaffa Cake to court they did. Of all the things.

The only way out for McVitie's was to prove that the Jaffa Cake was indeed just that.

Value Added Tax on chocolate-covered *biscuits*, but none what-so-ever on chocolate-covered *cakes*.

Violet Incredible.

Leonard Long and the short of it is: biscuits go soft when they're stale. Cakes, on the other hand, of course –

Violet Go hard.

Leonard McVitie's presented the tribunal with a week-old cake-size Jaffa Cake – imagine that, eh? – with a week-old cake-size Jaffa Cake, showed it to them. Hard as you like.

That was that.

. . .

I made some sandwiches.

Violet Oh.

Leonard There's some ham and some cheese.

Violet Thank you.

Leonard Would you like one now?

Violet Fine for the moment, actually, thank you.

Leonard Well, you just let me know.

. . .

Violet Would you mind if I used your bathroom?

Leonard Up the stairs, first left. Depending on how much of a rush you're in, feel free to use the stair lift.

Exit Violet.

48

Leonard moves close to a mirror hung on the wall.
He checks his teeth for food in the mirror.
He straightens his tie.
Enter Violet.

All right?

Violet Thank you.

Leonard The flush was all right, was it?

Violet . . .

Leonard The flush: all right, was it?

. . .

Thank you for coming.

Violet Not at all.

Leonard Train was all right, was it?

Violet Sorry?

Leonard Train: all right, was it?

Violet It was fine, yes.

Leonard Been a couple of very serious accidents affecting some of the local trains recently, that's all.

Violet I saw.

. . .

It's a lovely house, isn't it?

Leonard What's that?

Violet (*louder*) It's a lovely house.

Leonard There's some sheltered accommodation along the way.

Violet Oh, really?

Leonard Just down the way there.
  Wasn't sure about it myself.
  Some people rave about it.
  Seem a nice bunch.
  Have a fish-and-chip night once a Tuesday.
  Try and pop along as and when I've got the time.

. . .

Why don't I go and get us a couple of those sandwiches?

Violet smiles a little.
  Exit Leonard.
  Violet looks around the room, taking it in a little more.
  She is perhaps a little taken aback by the room's decay.
  Enter Leonard with two small plates of sandwiches cut into quarters, a bottle of red wine and a particularly modern-looking corkscrew.

You're not a vegetarian, are you?

Violet No.

Leonard Well, the pink ones are ham, just so you know.

Violet Thank you.

Leonard Would you like some wine?

Violet Are you sure?

Leonard Of course.
  Now watch this, you'll like this.

Leonard readies himself to open the bottle of wine with the corkscrew.

Seen one of these before? (*Corkscrew.*)

Violet Can't say that I have, no.

Leonard Ninety pounds these go for.

Violet Goodness.

Leonard Nickel. Top quality.
You just put it on –

Leonard places the corkscrew on top of the bottle of wine.

– and pull the . . .

Leonard struggles somewhat with the corkscrew.

None of this –

Violet Are you all right?

Leonard (*still struggling*) It's simple.
None of this –

Violet We don't have to have wine.

Leonard continues to struggle for a moment.

Leonard.

Leonard gives up, his frustration growing.

Leonard Normally, the.
Normally you see, you just.

Leonard tries the corkscrew again but still has no luck with it.
He looks around the room.
He moves to a unit in the room – a coffee table or something similar – and smashes the top of the bottle of wine open.

Violet Leonard.

Leonard There we are, look.

Violet ?!

Leonard Forgot the glasses.
Would you mind nipping into the kitchen?

Violet shakes her head a little.
  She exits.
  Leonard puts the broken wine bottle down and perhaps shakes any spilt wine from his hands, wipes his hands on his clothing etc.
  Enter Violet with two glasses and a roll of kitchen paper.
  Violet begins trying to clean up the wine with the kitchen paper.

Please. Don't worry about that.

Violet It'll stain if we don't –

Leonard Please.
Carpet's older than I am.
Please.

Violet stops attempting to clean the wine.
  Leonard pours a drink for Violet and himself.
  He hands Violet a glass of wine.

Cheers.

Violet smiles, the beginnings of laughter.
  Leonard and Violet toast.
  Both drink. It's disgusting. Violet in particular is surprised by just how disgusting it is.

Blimey.

Violet Yes.

Leonard It's a bit.

Violet It is.

Leonard Battery acid springs to mind.
It was on special. Three for two.

There's two more underneath the stairs.

Violet laughs a little.

Maybe you could take one with you?

Violet Or maybe we'll just have to save it for next time?

. . .

Leonard How was the train?

Violet It was fine.

Leonard Good.

. . .

So I bought your book.

Violet . . .

Leonard Upstairs, by the bed.
  Big.

Violet (*smiling*) Is it?

Leonard What-d'ya-call-it? Weapon of Mass Destruction.

Violet Sorry?

Leonard Size of it.

Violet I see.

Leonard Great big thing it is.

Violet Yes.
  Sorry about that.

Leonard Tiny words though, what gets me.

Violet How do you mean?

Leonard Words, on the page, tiny aren't they?

Violet Are they?

Leonard Bugger to read, you know.

Violet . . .

Leonard Not started it yet, have to confess.
  'S next on the old list, though.

Violet You'll have to let me know what you think.

Leonard I will.

Violet What are you reading at the moment?

Leonard Luck it was really, wasn't it?

Violet I'm sorry?

Leonard Luck.
  Us.
  Your book.

Violet I see, yes.

Leonard I said to you, didn't I? How it was that I came
across it.

Violet You did, yes.

Leonard Doctor's surgery, those magazines, those
magazines they have lying around.
  Flicking through, interview.
  I thought, 'No. Can't be.'
  There it all was.
  Bath. The shop.
  Y' husband.
  Couldn't believe it.

. . .

Said you were short-listed?

Violet That's right. I was.

Leonard Short-listed.

(*Meaning sandwiches.*) All right, are they?

Violet Lovely.

Leonard Rare-breed pork that is.
Best you'll find.

Leonard watches Violet.

I'm sorry.

Violet Whatever for?

Leonard Going on.

Violet Don't be silly.

Leonard I'm rambling.

Violet Not at all.

Leonard What's that?

Violet (*louder*) I was saying there's –

Leonard Nervous. Started shaking like a leaf when I heard that taxi.

Violet Well, you mustn't be.

. . .

Leonard Rain's unbelievable.
Washed away if we're not careful.
. . .
I was sorry to read about your husband. In that article.

Violet They actually. They made a mistake actually.

Leonard Oh?

Violet In the article.
He actually. Jack. He actually had his first stroke before retiring. And it was only then, following his retirement, that he had his second.

I asked my agent about it. About getting it corrected.
But she said that it happens all the time. In the press.
She said that it happens all the time.
Would you mind if I had another Jaffa Cake?

Leonard Course not.

Violet Thank you.

Leonard offers Violet the box of Jaffa Cakes.
Violet eats.

Leonard So how'd you –?
How'd you get into all this.
Writing.

Violet It was after the children left home.
It was Jack's suggestion. My husband –

Leonard Yes.

Violet Sorry, of course you – (*Doesn't finish: 'know who Jack is.'*)
I'm too old to study, I said.
Rubbish, he said. Nonsense.
In fact – and I don't know if this is the sort of thing that you might be interested in, but – a number of us, in Bath, we're trying to put together a proposal.
For a . . . memorial.

Leonard I don't live in Bath.

Violet No, I know, I know, of course, but.
I don't know, I suppose I thought that perhaps –

Leonard Live here, Violet –

Violet No, I know. I know.

Leonard Luton.

Violet I meant perhaps that I could let you know how we're getting on. From time to time.

If you. If that was something that you thought you might like to hear about. I could.

We're hoping to have the names of everyone who was killed during the raids on Bath engraved on to a, well, on to a.

It'll be just over four hundred names.

. . .

Why don't you – You could just let me know your thoughts once you've had a chance to look through the book perhaps.

(*Meaning she's rambling, in reference to Leonard's comment earlier.*) Now who's going on?

Leonard (*shakes his head a little*) . . .

Violet Leonard –

Violet's mobile telephone begins to ring, loud, volume as high as it goes.
She immediately begins rummaging through her handbag.

I'm so sorry.

Violet finds her mobile telephone and rejects the call.

Leonard If you need to answer it.

Violet It's just Emily. My daughter.

Leonard There's a phone by the front door if you'd like to use it.

Violet It's fine.

Leonard Cordless.

Violet Let me turn it off.

Leonard She'll be worried.

Violet Would you mind if I just send her a text message?

Leonard Of course not.

Violet It could take a while.

Leonard Why don't I go for a ride on the stairs and leave you to it?

> *Exit Leonard.*
> *Violet sends her daughter a text message.*
> *The wind outside howls, tapping almost at the windows. The rain continues to hammer down also. The light in the room flickers briefly.*
> *Violet finishes sending the text message.*
> *Enter Leonard.*

Do you not have hands-free?

Violet I'm sorry?

Leonard Great they are. Hands-free.
Attach it to your ear. Keep it on all day if needs be.

Violet . . .

Leonard How is she anyway?

Violet ?

Leonard Your daughter.

Violet Sorry.

Leonard Keeping well is she?

Violet She is.

Leonard Must be, what?

Violet She's fifty-one.

Leonard Fifty-one. My goodness.
Married is she?

Violet Yes.

Leonard And do we approve?

Violet . . .

Leonard Oh dear.

Violet No –

Leonard Oh dear, oh dear.

Violet No, he's lovely –

Leonard Lovely, oh dear.

Violet No, he really is.

Leonard But.

Violet You mustn't tell a soul.

Leonard zips his mouth.

. . .
He works for Durex.
They make –

Leonard I know what they make.

Violet He's nice enough.
Oh, I feel terrible now –

Leonard Don't be silly.

Violet It's simply.
It's simply that I find it rather difficult to get all that excited about.

Leonard About?

Violet Sex.

Leonard and Violet perhaps laugh a little between themselves.

Leonard What about your son?

Violet No longer with us unfortunately.

Leonard Oh, Violet –

Violet Oh, no, sorry, he, he. He lives in Australia. Brisbane.
Settled out there years ago.
Have you ever been?

Leonard nods.

Violet To Australia?

Leonard To Australia.

Violet How wonderful, when were you there?

Leonard A very, very long time ago.

Violet watches Leonard.

Violet I have to confess to you, Leonard, I've been feeling curiously nervous all day.
I had a gin on the train.
And then I had another but then I started to feel a little squiffy so I bought a packet of crisps and I ate them in one of the vestibules.
I made the taxi driver drive around and around.
I'm sorry, I said, but I don't think I'm actually quite ready yet, would you mind just –
I'll pay, I said. Of course I'll pay.
I was excited and then I was nervous and then I felt excited again and then I became anxious.
We've a lot to cover really, haven't we?

Leonard . . .

Violet How are you, Leonard?

Leonard . . .
(*Sandwiches.*) I could, could always pop some of these on the grill.

Got one of these, one of these George Foremans.
Incredible they are.

Violet . . .

Leonard Does everything.
Bacon, chicken. Sandwiches.

Violet I'm fine, thank you.

Leonard Can have a look later if you want?

Violet At George Foreman?

Leonard That's right.

Violet He's out there in the kitchen, is he?

Leonard That's right. Big fella he is, but we try and
squeeze him in underneath the sink when we can.
(*Calling to George Foreman as if he were in the
kitchen.*) All right, George?

*Leonard and Violet smile a little.
He offers her the plate of sandwiches.*

Please.

*Violet takes a sandwich.
Violet and Leonard each eat a sandwich.
Leonard coughs a little.
Violet watches.
Leonard continues to cough.*

Violet Would you like a glass of water?

*Leonard gestures, waves, 'No thank you,' and
continues to cough.
Violet watches.*

Leonard, why don't I go and get you –

*Leonard heaves and, along with a little sandwich,
coughs up a not insignificant amount of blood.*

He attempts to catch the blood in his hands.
Violet immediately pulls a handkerchief from her
pocket and moves to Leonard.
Leonard's coughing subsides.
Violet receives a text message.

Leonard (*his voice a little worn*) Do see to that if you
have to.

Violet Don't be silly.

Violet cleans Leonard's mouth, carefully and
systematically.
Leonard, finally, clears his throat.
The rain hammers against the window, the light in
the room flickers briefly.
Leonard and Violet, close.

Leonard Could I ask you to do something for me?

Violet . . .

Leonard It won't take long.

Violet . . .

Exit Leonard.
The wind outside continues to roar, the rain
hammering the window.
The light in the room flickers momentarily. Violet
looks up as it does so.
Enter Leonard.
Leonard carries an electronic keyboard and a stand
for it.
As Violet looks on, Leonard proceeds to set up the
keyboard, readying it for a song.
After a moment or two, when the keyboard is
ready:

Leonard, have you bought this?

Leonard It was in the sale. Reduced.

Violet How long have you had it?

Leonard gestures for Violet to take a seat behind the keyboard.

Leonard.

Leonard Please.

Leonard, again, gestures for Violet to take a seat behind the keyboard.

Violet What do you want me to play?

Leonard . . .

Violet You know my daughter, Emily, she said, she said that the idea of you and I, that the idea of us meeting one another, after all these years, she said that she thought it was completely and utterly ridiculous.

Why on earth do you want to do it, she said.

She actually got quite angry.

She'd never heard of you, you see. Until recently. Until very, very recently, she'd never even heard your name.

She found it very strange. The idea that I had been with someone before her father.

She would simply rather I left it all alone, I think.

You're obsessed, she said. The past.

It's not healthy, she said.

That's where you're wrong, I said.

It is vital.

It is absolutely vital.

Violet is perhaps growing a little upset.

I made a list, would you believe.

On the train. Don't forget to ask him about this, don't forget to ask him about that.

Questions.

And now don't take this the wrong way, Leonard, will you, but.

It strikes me that you have little to no desire to talk about anything at all.

But you contacted me, Leonard.

Do you understand?

Leonard If you need to get going –

Violet I wasn't –

Leonard If you wanted to make a move –

Violet Leonard, who looks after you?

Leonard, no one should have to spend all of their time on their own.

The light in the room flickers briefly.

Leonard Can I offer you another sandwich?

Violet No, thank you.

Leonard Clear all this up. (*Sandwiches etc.*)

He clears away sandwiches, glasses, wine bottle, etc., and exits.
   Violet takes a seat behind the keyboard.
   She tries a note.
   She tries another note.
   With a certain amount of uncertainty, Violet begins to play 'One Day When We Were Young'.
   The wind outside howls and the rain hammers against the window.
   Violet sings the first four verses of 'One Day When We Were Young' (from Oscar Hammerstein's lyrics for the film The Great Waltz). *Her voice is soft, delicate.*
   Then she plays an incorrect note. She tries again.

Violet 'When –'

Again, something isn't quite right. Violet stops.
Enter Leonard.

Leonard I had a flick through the photographs in your book. Couple of weeks ago.
There was one of that hotel, wasn't there?

Violet That's right.

Leonard Was it ever rebuilt?

Violet No. It's student accommodation now.
You can still see scorch marks on some of the other buildings. Scars.
May I show you something?

Leonard . . .

Violet moves to her handbag and takes out a letter, sealed in an envelope. The envelope is clearly fairly old, delicate.
Violet holds out the envelope for Leonard to take.

Violet You don't have to read it now.
You don't even have to read it, I suppose. But.
I would like to give it to you.

Leonard is hesitant.

(*The envelope.*) Please.

Leonard takes the envelope from Violet.
He hesitates.
*He goes to open the envelope. Suddenly, however –
as the storm outside peaks – there is a power cut and
the room is plunged into darkness.*

Leonard I'll just see if I can . . .

Exit Leonard.
*Violet moves to the light switch in the room and
tries it, flicks it up and down a few times.*

Enter Leonard with a handful of sparklers and a box of matches.

Might have to make do for the time being, I'm afraid.

Leonard hands a sparkler to Violet.
He lights a match.

Steady now.

Leonard lights Violet's sparkler, it burns into life.
He lights his sparkler using Violet's.
Slowly, their sparklers burn out. Perhaps, as the sparklers burn down, Leonard and Violet make shapes in the air, enjoying themselves a little.

I've been reading *The War of the Worlds*.
Spotted it at a car boot sale.
My mother used to read that to me, I thought.

Violet How are you finding it?

Leonard What's that?

Violet (*louder*) How are you finding it, are you enjoying it?

Leonard It's terrifying.

Power resumes, the light in the room explodes into life. For a moment perhaps, it is uncomfortably bright.
Slowly, the storm outside begins to subside until there is just a trickle of rain.

What was it that you wanted to ask?

Violet I'm sorry?

Leonard Earlier on, said you had a list.
Said that you'd made a list.

Violet That's right.
On the train, I was.
Anxious, I suppose.

Leonard Where did you want to start?

Violet . . .

Leonard We could take turns.
   I could start if you like?

Violet Okay.

Leonard . . .

   Violet watches Leonard.

Violet Leonard –

Leonard Thank you for coming.
   We should start there really.
   For coming to see me.
   Thank you.

   The rain outside continues to drizzle.